Praise for
LESSONS IN STALKING

"Dena Harris has written a cat book even a dog would love."
—Tim Bete, director of the Erma Bombeck Writers' Workshop and
author of *In the Beginning... There Were No Diapers*

"Captures perfectly the nuances of life with cats!"
—Rita Davis, Editor, *Cats & Kittens*

"Clever, witty, and insightful, these stories celebrate everything feline and bring smiles of recognition to anyone who loves cats. The author relates the charming antics of her loving, yet manipulative fur-kids, and shows how their c'attitude impacts humans with predictable—and often hilarious—results. Read one by one or devoured like a catnip toy, the stories in *Lessons In Stalking* are the purr-fect treat! I am a fan."
—Amy Shojai, nationally known authority on pet care and
behavior and author of multiple books including *PETiquette*
and coeditor of *Chicken Soup for the Cat Lover's Soul*

"Never has watching someone else own a cat been this much fun."
—Lisa Allmendinger, Editor, *I Love Cats!*

"Dena Harris magically captures the humor of sharing our lives with cats in a master storyteller's style. You catch yourself laughing out loud as you read her words filled with whimsy and wit. She is simply meow-val-lous!"
—Arden Moore, *Catnip* Editor and author of
The Kitten Owner's Manual

"If laughter is the best medicine, there's no telling how healthy you'll be after spending time with this hilarious book! Cat people will find echoes of their own experiences with the feline. And if you can walk past the refrigerator without a wary glance after reading "The Creature Under the Fridge," you're a braver soul than I!"
—Jean Hofve, DVM, holistic medicine practitioner

"This is the relationship 'how-to' book for cat owners. I recommend this book to any family or couple thinking of being owned by a cat. Nothing is funnier than the truth!"
—Janet Oquendo, VP Operations, Pet Lover's Connection, www.petloversconnection.com

"In these charming stories, Dena Harris shares with us her happy discoveries of cat nature in its many guises. This is a sweet book, filled with the author's delight not only in her two young cats, but also in her husband and her home."
—Marion Lane, Special Projects Editor, ASPCA National Programs Office

"Lessons In Stalking is for all cat lovers! Each story in this collection is a little gem...colored with a multi-faceted understanding of our feline friends...sparkling with the kitty humor that we all recognize and love...and polished with that passionate devotion to cats common to each of us."
—Ellen Price, Managing Editor, *The World of Professional Pet Sitting*

"Dena Harris is very funny."
—Annie, 11 years old, in a letter to the editor of *Cats & Kittens* magazine

"Despite what you may have heard, cats are funny. They're comedians, in fact, beginning in kittenhood with acrobatic slapstick. Adult cats enjoy more subtle forms of humor which, as Dena Harris makes as obvious as a toy mouse in a water bowl, promote us mere humans from lowly food servers in the kitty cafeteria to royal fools in the feline court. Harris is a funny lady with a hilarious take on the life of doting cat parents and their band of furry funsters. We may as well laugh at ourselves—our cats certainly do!"
—Sheila Webster Boneham, Ph.D., Author of *The Complete Idiot's Guide to Getting and Owning a Cat*

Lessons
in Stalking

Lessons in Stalking

Lessons in Stalking

Adjusting to Life With Cats

Dena Harris

Spotlight Publishing, Inc. • Madison, North Carolina

Lessons in Stalking
Adjusting to Life With Cats

by Dena Harris

Published by:
> Spotlight Publishing, Inc.
> P. O. Box 621
> Madison, North Carolina
> 27025-0621

Printed in the United States of America

ISBN 0-9768469-2-6
LCCN 2005905157

This book is dedicated to
LUCY
who started it all.

Acknowledgements

A big "thumbs up" to the Universe for all the cool cats out there—nicely done.

Many thanks to all my writer friends who managed to smile through gritted teeth when I asked if they would mind reading "just one more cat story?" Special thanks to Tom Truitt, Betsy O'Brien Harrison, "Maddie," Sally, Kaptain, Cherie, and all the writers at The Writer's Way who encouraged me. Plus, hats off to all members of the Cat Writer's Association (CWA) who remind me I'm not alone in my maniacal devotion to cats.

A big thank you to Rita Davis, editor of *Cats & Kittens* magazine where many of these stories first appeared. She said she couldn't hire me as a humor columnist then proceeded to publish my stories in the magazine's humor column for the next two years. (Ha ha! I win!)

Love to my family, who remind me daily they think I'm the coolest thing since sliced bread.

And a tremendous and loving thank you to my husband, the most patient, tolerant, encouraging, and supportive human being on the planet. Thanks for letting me write the stories so it always looks like I'm right.

Finally, love to my feline babies Lucy & Olivia for providing hours of entertainment and fodder for this book. I know as I write this chances are you're both doing something really hideous to my chairs, but I love you anyway.

Table of Contents

PART II: Cat and Kitten

Preface

It's happened. I have become *that* woman. The one obsessed with cats. Friends no longer put any thought into purchasing gifts for me. If it has a cat on it, they figure (correctly) that I'll love it. That's how it starts. People start thinking this way and soon—through no fault of your own—you're living in a house filled with cat picture frames, cat gloves, cat bookmarks, cat plaques, cat mugs, and yes, even cat underwear.

How cool is that?

We couldn't have cats growing up because my dad was allergic. We discovered this when we actually *had* a cat for a few months. Notice the few months part. I inherited my love of cats from my mom and for a while it was a tough call on who would have to leave, Dad or the cat. (Dad won by a nose hair because he didn't shed on the couch.)

So I couldn't wait to be an adult and have a cat of my own. But around age 18 I developed allergies. I practically blew up when I was around cats.

Desperate, I tried allergy shots but my allergist warned me I must "never, ever own a cat."

Then I met Lucy.

She was about three months old, a stray, and playing with a leaf outside a building. It was a November night before the first frost and no one would take her home. I couldn't bear the thought of leaving her.

"Hey," I said, "Do you want to come home with me?"

She abandoned her leaf, ran to me, put her tiny front paws on my leg, looked up and said, "Mew."

Well. I'm only human.

I packed her in my car and drove home. The look on my husband's face when I walked in the door was less one of surprise and more one of resignation. He'd seen this day coming.

"No, no," I said, cutting him off. "I know I can't keep her. It's just for a day or two until I find a home for her."

"Uh-huh," he said and left the house without another word. When he returned twenty minutes later it was with litter box, food, dishes, and play toys, which he set up in the special "Lucy corner."

He's a good man.

And he was right. Lucy never left. Amazingly, I had no allergic reaction to her whatsoever.

This is not true of all cats. Our kitten Olivia makes me sneeze (but she's so darn cute, I just suck it up).

Lucy is special. All cats are special. And it was obviously meant to be that I have cats in my life. I can't imagine our home without them.

I hope you have cats in your life. And if you're so inclined, feel free to send me a cat knick-knack for my home.

One can never have enough of these things.

Dena Harris
Madison, NC
April, 2005

Part I
The Cat

Feline Concerns

-1-
Feline Concerns

I'm worried about the cat. She keeps dropping mice into her water dish. I don't think that's normal. We wake one morning to find a small, red cotton mouse floating face-down in the dish. We figure she accidentally batted it in there. We set it on the side of the sink to dry out. The next morning, we find another one floating. Then another that evening and two more by morning. I mention my concerns to my husband.

"Something's wrong with the cat. I don't think it's normal to keep putting mice in a water dish. Do you think she's acting out? Like an act of aggression?"

"Maybe she just likes putting mice in her water dish," he counters.

I grimace at him. "No, she must be upset about something. This is her way of trying to communicate. What do you think she could be upset about?"

"That we keep taking the mice *out* of the water dish?" he offers.

I stop talking to him about it and instead watch the cat for clues.

She grows bolder in her moves. While she used to wait for us to go to bed or to work before drowning the mice, we now begin finding wet mice where moments before there were none. Walking back to the kitchen on a commercial break, we stop and stare at the water dish.

"Look, there's another one," says my husband.

"I can see that," I say. "I told you she was upset."

He continued on to the kitchen. "I'm not touching it then."

I try talking to her about it. "Sweet-ums, why are you putting your mice in the water?"

She looks at me with perfectly round eyes.

"What's the matter? Tell Mommy." I reach out to hold her, but she bounds away.

I'm sure her hostility is directed at us and is no reflection toward the mice themselves. They have always been her favorite. We bring home a bag of five each month, and she goes crazy with delight, batting them around on our hardwood floors.

And where have all those mice gone? If we calculate bringing home five mice a month for six months, that's thirty mice somewhere in our home. I can today account for the whereabouts of approximately three. I suspect foul play.

I speak to my mom who says, "She wants attention. That's her way of telling you."

"But Mom, I already pay her attention! I pet her every morning, and we play when I get home from work, and I pet her at dinner and before we go to bed."

"Well then, maybe she's trying to tell you to leave her alone."

I cross Mom off the list of people I will discuss this with.

Then, as suddenly as they appeared, the wet mice vanish. No more floating cotton corpses. I watch the cat carefully, but nothing seems to have changed. She still likes playing with them, and she still runs from me when I try to pet her. But she is no longer drowning mice.

I hope this is a good thing. I mention to my husband that I am concerned about the cat because she is no longer drowning her mice. He stares at me in disbelief before throwing up his hands and leaving the room.

I suppose he's right.

Maybe there never was a problem after all?

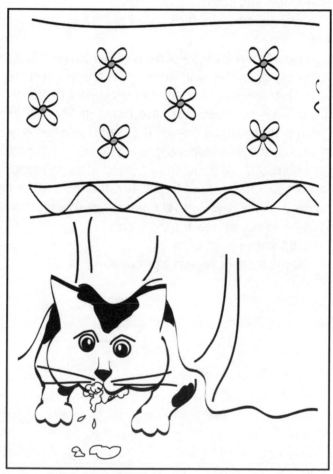

Never Feed A Cat Grape Benadryl®

-2-

Never Feed A Cat Grape Benadryl®

It's a horrible feeling of helplessness and responsibility, tending to a sick pet. When examining an ailing animal, it's vital one be calm, levelheaded, and not concede to over-reaction.

Luckily, I'm one of those rare individuals able to remain composed in the face of any emergency.

I demonstrated this skill when our cat became ill. We heard her firing off bazooka-rounds of sneezes. My husband and I came on the run. I took charge.

"Oh my God, she's dying!" I wailed, flinging myself on the cat and wrapping her in a stifling embrace. "Dying!" I started to cry.

My husband ran a slow hand down his face. "Maybe she just has a cold," he offered.

I raised a bewildered cat to eye level. "Tell Mommy where it hurts."

My husband took the cat from me and examined her eyes, ears, and nose. "It's probably just a cold," he reassured. "We'll call the vet tomorrow."

I remained doubtful but the cat was now hiding under the sofa, consciously suppressing her sneezes.

I called the vet first thing in the morning.

"Hello-I-have-an-emergency," I said.

"Yes ma'am?"

"It's my cat. She keeps sneezing."

"Yes ma'am," she said.

I remained silent, awaiting instructions.

Finally figuring out I expected her to say something else, the receptionist continued. "Um, is there any vomiting or diarrhea?"

My God, is this woman stupid? I would have had the cat at the emergency hospital at the first sign of vomiting or diarrhea. I took a deep breath and reminded myself to speak slowly, so she could understand me.

"No, it's just sneezing. But it's a lot of sneezing. She sneezed twenty times in a row. For five minutes straight."

I waved away my husband who was trying to take the phone. As an accountant he has this hang-up about accurate numbers. I felt it more important to convey the gravity of the situation.

Dire possibilities, each worse than the one before, occurred to me. I burst forth with one nightmare scenario.

"Do you think she might be having an allergic reaction?" I asked. "Maybe she has internal hives? I saw her scratching her ear earlier. How exactly would I treat internal cat hives?"

The receptionist did the only thing she could do, which was to put me on hold. She spoke cautiously when she returned.

"Ma'am, it sounds like an upper respiratory infection. Pick up some alcohol-free liquid Benadryl® and give your cat one milliliter per pound of body weight.* If that doesn't do the trick in a few days, call us back."

"Fine," I muttered and hung up. No one cared that my cat was at death's door. Even my husband was useless, tossing balls down the hall for the cat to chase. She was stoic enough to pretend to enjoy the diversion.

I trudged to the store and came back with the Benadryl®.

"Grape?" my husband asked, examining the bottle.

"It was that or bubble-gum. Let's just get it down her."

He scooped up the cat, and I positioned the dropper in her mouth. One hour, three new droppers, and half a bottle of wasted medication later, we managed to get about an eighth of a teaspoon down her throat. She fled as soon as we released her. I went in pursuit to offer my apologies. I don't care for grape flavor myself.

When I found the cat, my heart flip-flopped. There was white foam bubbling from her mouth. Even my husband paled.

"Call the vet," he said.

I raced to the phone and dialed with trembling fingers. I explained our beloved cat was now foaming at the mouth. The receptionist giggled. I mentally planned how I would kill her.

"Oh, I forgot to tell you," she said. "Benadryl® makes a lot of cats foam at the mouth. Don't worry about it."

---

* Never give your pet medication without first consulting your vet. Benadryl® is not intended for feline consumption.

"Benadryl® makes a lot of cats foam at the mouth, but you didn't think to mention that to me?" I wanted to be sure I had the facts right for my trial.

The receptionist sighed. "If it will make you feel better, why don't you bring the cat in and we'll take a look at her."

I brought the cat in and the vet ran some tests. "Looks like a head cold," he said. "I'm going to give you a prescription for something a lot like Benadryl®. That ought to knock it out."

My husband greeted me at the door as I returned. "What did the vet say?" he asked.

"He said the cat has a cold," I said. My husband smiled. "Not a word," I warned.

He left without saying anything, but I heard him telling the cat it was now safe to sneeze.

He thinks he's funny but I'll have the last laugh.

The next time he gets a cold, I'm going to feed him the rest of the Grape Benadryl®.

Never Feed A Cat Grape Benadryl®

Lessons In Stalking

-3-

Lessons In Stalking

She's stalking us again. It makes me nervous. Not the stalking part, but the fact that she doesn't seem to be very good at it.

She stalks us right out in the open, inching toward us on her stomach in the middle of the hallway.

"What's she doing?" my husband asks, looking over his shoulder. "Is she sick?"

"Shhhh!" I reprimand. "She's stalking us. Be supportive."

"But I don't want to be stalked," he whines.

"She needs to learn. Now act surprised when she pounces."

Attacks are generally mild. A quick paw to the foot, a snatch at a pants leg and she's off.

Sometimes she'll stalk us from behind the sofa. It's not a bad ploy, except we can see her tail sticking out. I draw her attention, while my husband sneaks up behind her.

"BOO!" he yells, jabbing at her hindquarters.

It may seem harsh, but she has to learn.

We're not her only prey. She also stalks the plaid cotton mice we procure for her. She'll spy one resting in the hall. Every muscle tenses as she flattens herself on the floor, tail flicking. Body rigid, she's a tightly wound coil.

When the moment comes—did the mouse twitch?—she leaps into the air. We watch her descend, fangs and claws bared in case of counterattack.

Then she's on top of the mouse, spearing it with her teeth, viciously shaking her head. She notices us watching her and freezes. Snatching the mouse, she bounds away.

"Well done sweetheart! " I cheer. I elbow my husband.

"Uh, way to go," he stammers. "You the cat." He glares at me.

"She's not going to improve unless she's told what she's doing right," I explain calmly. "It's called positive reinforcement."

He walks away mumbling under his breath.

Although the cotton mice are fun, we find the cat truly enjoys moving targets. We discover this when a fly gets into our home.

The cat is all business. Darting eyes, shortness of breath, bushy tail—as she stalks the fly I think that she's finally coming in to her own.

But then, "Click-aaack-aaack-claaack." Dolphin-like sounds emanate from her throat as she sits with arched back, staring at the fly buzzing above her.

My husband races in. "What was that?"

"That's the cat."

"What's she doing? "he asks. "Is she sick?"

"Maybe," I say.

I question whether our cat will ever get the hang of this stalking business. My husband and I grow weary of acting surprised every time we're attacked. The fly went on to lead a long and happy life. My hopes center again on the cotton mice. And I just saw several of them lying, almost hidden, behind the couch.

I think they're waiting to jump out and yell "BOO!"

The Big Brown Mouse & Other Toys Our Cat Loathes

-4-

The Big Brown Mouse & Other Toys Our Cat Loathes

We sat the big brown mouse in the middle of the kitchen floor. The cat looked on disinterestedly. The mouse was a gift from our pet sitter; a sweet elderly woman who I'm sure had no idea the trauma her gift was about to induce.

"The mouse has a little switch in its back," the pet sitter informed us. Flipping the switch caused the mouse to move about in motorized circles on the floor.

"Your cat will love it," she assured us. "All cats love it."

Our cat most certainly did *not* love it. When we flipped the switch, a great tremor enveloped the room as the mouse's internal gaskets roared to life. We set the mouse on the floor and it raced about in jerky circles. Fast jerky circles. In fact, the mouse appeared to have overdosed on some form of an illegal substance.

Not that the cat would know this. She disappeared from the room at the first sign of life from the mouse. We found her an hour later, trembling under an upstairs bed.

We decided the motor and the presence of a big brown mouse was too much to take in all at once. We agreed we needed to "introduce" the cat to the mouse—as if they might agree to meet later for drinks if they hit it off.

The next night at dinner my husband retrieved the mouse and placed it again in the center of the kitchen floor, where it stayed for several hours.

The cat wouldn't come near it.

I tried getting down on the floor and petting the mouse, to show the cat there was no danger. She looked even more alarmed at these actions. Perhaps she thought I was thinking of trading her in.

On the second night she acquiesced, somewhat, and agreed to be in the same room with the mouse. She sat atop a chair and didn't take her eyes off the brown monstrosity. Out of pity, I hid the mouse before we went to bed. I don't think the cat would have slept otherwise.

Night three was the same. The mouse was on the floor; the cat was on the chair. She left briefly to use the facilities, as my husband insists on referring to the litter box.

"This is stupid," he said after she left the room. "She obviously hates that thing. Let's get rid of it."

I balked at giving up on yet another toy. After all, I had been the one to throw out the parrot on a suction cup that stuck to doors and "soared lifelike about your cat's head," promising hours of fun.

The cat never looked up.

I took back the catnip filled Garfield toys, the cat spa, and toys with random glitter and feathers stuck to them, all purchased in the hopes of enticing my feline to play.

She sniffed them once and walked away.

And let's not forget the eighty-five dollar kitty jungle gym with carpet more plush than is to be found anywhere in *my* home, that was a "must" for indoor cats.

The cat climbed it once to prove she could and now won't go near it except to occasionally sharpen her claws. We use it as a plant holder.

But even I, who had envisioned hours of fun for the cat that didn't involve me having to stand in one place and swat around a plastic fishing pole with rubber-fly lure attached, had to agree. The cat was just not getting into the spirit of things. I got up and threw the mouse away.

The cat walked into the kitchen to rejoin us and froze. Eyes darting, her body language spoke as plainly as words: *Where the heck did that thing go?*

She was obviously terrified. She crouched low and peered under the table, searching for the mouse. Nothing. She slowly raised her head and examined what she could see of the table and chairs. Nothing. A bird chirped outside and the cat leaped, hissing.

"I feel bad," I told my husband. "She's still freaked out."

"Yeah, maybe we should buy her a new toy," he said. "You know, something to distract her. I'll see what I can find."

The toy he came back with looked harmless enough— a musical ball that played various songs from the musical "Cats" every time it was nudged. The cat adores it, if only because she knows we're slowly going insane.

She has us living on edge. We're at the point where she was when she was freaked out about the brown mouse. We cling to the edge of our chairs, bleary-eyed from lack of sleep, swatting at shadows, afraid everything that moves might start to play "Mr. Mistoffolees."

And the cat is laughing. She even goes so far as to occasionally hide the ball so we may experience the fear of never knowing exactly when we might be attacked by a bright blue orb winging down the hall screeching "Memory" at full volume.

But we'll have the last laugh. We're going out of town again and invited the pet sitter back. And we made sure to tell her how much the cat *loved* her gift and to please bring another.

Between the musical orb and the motorized brown mouse, I'll take the mouse.

I have to.

My nerves can't take any more.

Yoga Cat

-5-

Yoga Cat

I took up yoga two years ago, around the same time we got our cat. Having read that owning a cat and practicing yoga were both fail-safe methods to soothe troubled nerves, I envisioned a life filled with peace and inner reflection.

Now two years wiser, I know that people who own cats do yoga simply to release the stress in their lives that exists because they own a cat.

My cat mocks me while I do yoga. As I sit on my padded blue mat, tangled up in a pose the human body, or at least *my* body, was not meant to perform, she'll sit beside me and perform the same pose flawlessly.

"Now, raise your right leg, keeping your left leg fully extended," coos my video yoga instructor. "Balance on your sitting bones, and raise the leg over your head."

Puffing and grunting, I try to extend my leg. Without breaking a sweat, the cat plops herself down beside me and raises her right leg over her head, making sure her back leg remains fully extended. I look over at her. She looks back and, pointedly, bends down and licks herself without lowering the leg.

I find this insulting.

I decide I need more personalized instruction and sign up at our local Y, paying $75 to have a certified yoga instructor twist me into painful and humiliating poses. But the cat is not there, executing a better version of "Downward Facing Dog" than me, so it's bearable.

"You're doing very well," encourages my instructor.

"Thank you," I say. "I'm trying to impress my cat."

The instructor backs away, and avoids me for the rest of the class. But I don't mind. I am raising and extending my legs at an advanced rate. I can't wait to show the cat.

I return home and pull out my mat. The cat looks pleased. It's been a few days since she's humiliated me.

"Ha! That's only what you think is going to happen," I say. "Watch this!" I proceed to execute a flawless "Dead-bug" pose. The cat looks amused.

"That's not all," I say. "I can also do this!" I move into Downward Facing Dog, remembering to *breathe*, as my instructor said.

The cat ambles over, takes a seat next to my head, and stares at me. My arms begin to tremble, but I refuse to give up the pose. The cat continues to stare, glancing significantly at my now shaking torso. I am no longer breathing properly. In fact, I think I am close to hyperventilating. The cat begins to purr.

I can't go any further. I collapse onto the mat. I'm pretty sure I've strained something. I can't locate exactly where at the moment, because my entire body is trembling.

Now that I'm on the floor, the cat yawns and stretches, fully extending her front legs and arching her back. She holds the pose. And holds it. And holds it. And darn it all, she's *breathing.* Releasing the pose, she takes a deep cleansing breath. Her final word on the subject is to claw at my yoga mat before exiting the room.

The phone rings. It's my yoga instructor.

"I was wondering if you wanted to sign up for our next series of classes," she said. "You were making such good progress."

I think about the physical anguish, and sweat, of the yoga class. Then I ponder the money spent to experience this pain. I tell the instructor I will not be returning to class. If it's pain I'm after, I can get that at home for free.

I'll just do yoga with my cat.

Kitty Chow

-6-

Kitty Chow

I am engaged in a battle of will against my cat. The upsetting part is that I'm losing.

Here's the scenario. While batting her food around one day (because apparently we can't *eat* it until first we've *stalked* it), the cat accidentally swatted a kibble into her water dish. That was good for about three minutes of fun as she sprayed water all over the kitchen floor in an attempt to remove the food. When she tired of seeing me on my hands and knees with a towel, she finally used her paw to scoop the food out of the dish and onto her mat. Then she ate it.

Of course "she ate it" is an understatement. Could she speak, the cat would say the skies opened and the heavens sang. We don't feed our cats moist food because I don't want to deal with half-used cans of smelly cat food in my fridge. (They might overpower the odor of the half-used cans of smelly human food we keep in there). But having discovered the joys of moistened food, there was no going back.

In fact, the cat liked the wet food so much, she now refuses to eat her food until we pour it into her water bowl, let it soak for about 20 seconds, and then dump it...where? Back into the food dish? Oh no, too easy.

No, the watery mess must be poured onto the food mat, in the exact place where she first discovered the delightful delicacy of kitty-chow con aqua.

If we pour it back in the dish, she won't eat it. If she doesn't see us dump the food in the water (I tried to save time and just wet the food at the sink), she won't eat it. Her Highness is very particular. And though I try to resist, I can't stand to see her not eat so I give in.

This isn't the first time I've caved. Early on, the cat insisted on stalking her food. This wouldn't have been so bad if she were an outdoor or barn cat with an ample supply of field mice and squirrels to keep her busy. What made the situation awkward is that she is an indoor cat, and the food she was stalking was IAMS® Indoor Cat Formula at almost fifteen dollars per two-pound bag.

She refused to eat the food unless we threw it across the floor, allowing her the opportunity to leap and pounce before savagely ripping the kibble to pieces. Sometimes she'd bat the kibbles across the floor and chase them. Other times, she'd run and hide beneath a kitchen chair, tail flinching to and fro, planning the moment of her attack.

My husband has no patience for this sort of behavior. If I dare complain that I am tired of throwing food across the floor or staring at wet cat chow on the mat, I am harassed with, "Well, what do you expect? You baby her way too much. If you just leave the food in the dish she'll eventually get hungry and eat it."

And he has a point. I mean, what's wrong with me that I bend so easily to the will of a fifteen-pound cat?

The answer is simple. I do it because she's cute. And she purrs really loud when I dump the food in the water, and even louder when she sees me scoop it onto the mat. Seriously, how many chances in life do you get to make someone *that* happy?

When I point this out my husband just stares at me. "You're nuts," is the only counterargument I receive. From this I conclude I have won our war of verbal sparring. In triumph, I toss the cat a kibble across the floor.

Still, I admit I'd like to be able to just pour the cat food in the bowl and move on with life. My husband insists he can help me wean the cat toward accepting our feeding rules; those being that the cat food goes in the bowl, dry, and stays there. Needless to say, the cat is not pleased with these new rules, which she vocalizes loudly.

"Mrow?" (Translation: *What's going on? Why is the food in my dish?*)

"Mrow? Rowr? Mrow?" (*Hello? Anyone? Hello?*)

"Mrow? Rowr, meow. Mo-ow??" (*Lady, get it in gear. I don't eat out of a dish. Re-mem-ber??*)

Receiving no response she resorts to bad language.

"ROWR-FSST?!?"

At this I throw a pleading glance at my husband. He doesn't even look up from his paper. "Ignore it," he says, turning the page.

I do ignore it. At least until he leaves the house. The cat and I both watch him pull his car down the drive. She looks at me.

"Wait for it," I say. My husband honks his horn good-bye. The cat looks at me again, ears perked. I give her the nod. "Yup, we're clear," I say. "Let's go for it."

And so I spend the next ten minutes feeding a deliriously happy cat a combination of wet cat food and hallway dust bunnies. The dust bunnies are an unintentional side effect of eating off the hardwood floors. My cleaning needs some work.

But I'm not going to dust my floors just for a cat.

I have to take a stand somewhere.

Kitty Chow

Incoming!

-7-

Incoming!

The cat has discovered a love of pasta. She prefers Mueller's® pasta shells, uncooked, of the medium-sized variety.

I inadvertently began her love affair with pasta by reaching into the kitchen cabinet for some soup. My elbow bumped an open box and dry pasta shells went scattering and bouncing across the tile floor.

I started, the cat jumped, and then we looked across the room at one another. Our eyes narrowed to slits. We both knew exactly what the other wanted. Without a word we went racing in opposite directions—me for the broom, the cat directly for the pile of shells.

It was no contest. By the time I arrived with the broom, she was in the middle of what appeared to be a free-for-all hockey shoot-out where, instead of a black puck, the cat was lobbing Mueller's® shells. She went down the line like a professional, nailing shot after shot.

ZAP! There went one into the dining room.

ZING! There went one under the stove (Add it to the list of things she's batted under there never to be retrieved).

POW! She was bouncing them off the fridge. She turned towards me, armed and ready, and I knew I must regain control.

"Hold it!" I command. "These are not toys! This is food your father and I require for our daily survival." I dangle one of her pom-pom balls in front of me. "Here, sweetie. Do you want to play with this?"

BAM! The cat wings a shell past my left ear.

That's it. No more Mrs. Nice Guy. I scoop up a yowling cat and deposit her in the bathroom, door closed. I go back and sweep up all the pasta now scattered throughout the house that I can find. It's really hard to reach the ones that went all the way under the couch.

Once finished, I let a very miffed cat out of her cell. She sniffs the floor where the pasta had been and turns toward me. I watch her consider her options. She decides to play the cuteness card.

Perfectly round eyes of innocence follow my every move. *I was just having fun. Is that so wrong? After all, I never even get to leave the house.*

I cross my arms over my chest. Seeing I am not to be moved, she heaves a theatrical sigh, drops her tail, and meanders away.

Later that afternoon, I start giggling. She did look pretty cute, happily whapping the beejeezus out of those shells.

I could have saved a heck of a lot of money, not to mention floor space, on cat toys if I'd known earlier the entertainment value of a fresh pasta shell.

My husband arrives home a couple of hours later. "What's that racket?" he asks. Indeed, there are suspicious sounds coming from behind the closed kitchen door.

"That's just the cat," I say. "She's playing."

"With what, firecrackers?" he asks.

"Um, I'm not sure. Listen, are you hungry? I was thinking we could eat out tonight."

He doesn't look excited. "But it's Tuesday. Pasta night."

I smile and listen to the ruckus in the kitchen as the cat gets off another hip shot. No pasta tonight.

I'm pretty sure we're out.

The Great Cat Butt Wiping Adventure

-8-

The Great Cat Butt Wiping Adventure

The cat smelled bad.

She no longer had the sweet, soft, fresh smell of well-groomed kitty fur. Now she smelled like ammonia. Or, in layman's terms, pee.

I mention the aroma to my husband.

"Are you cleaning the litter box?" I ask him. "Daily?"

"Why am I always the one who gets blamed?" he asks. "Why am I responsible for the cat smelling like pee?"

"Maybe she's sick," I say, cutting him off. "Let's keep an eye on her."

Worried, I hop on the Internet to do some research. Opening Google™, I enter my query: CATS SMELL URINE.

Five million sites on how to remove the smell of cat urine from carpets, furniture, suitcases, and clothing fill the screen.

I try again.

CATS SMELL FUR AMMONIA

CATS STINK URINE DISEASE

CATS SMELLY PEE DISEASE

Nothing, although I now know fifty different ways to remove urine stains from cashmere. I give it one last try.

CATS ICKY YUCK SMELL PROBABLY CAUSED BY HUSBANDS NON-SANITARY METHODS FOR FECES AND URINE CLUMP DISPOSAL

Bingo. A site for Feline Lower Urinary Tract Disease (FLUTD) appears. FLUTD, I read, takes on many different forms and stages. The most serious is when tiny crystals appear in a cat's urine. Death is possible.

I race downstairs where my husband is watching TV.

"Have you seen any signs of crystals?" I shriek.

"Huh?" he says.

"Fluted! Fatal cat disease! Crystals in the urine! Have you *seen* any?"

I race back upstairs, not giving him a chance to answer. The website indicates cats with urinary tract infections need to drink a lot of water, adding that with their inquisitive nature, cats are more likely to drink out of bowls placed in odd spots around the home. They also say some cats enjoy drinking from running water.

The next afternoon my husband approaches me.

"Why is my shower running?" he asks.

"In case the cat gets thirsty," I reply. "Can you move? You're blocking the TV."

Later that night he appears again, clenching a dripping sock in one hand.

"Did you know there's a pan full of water at the top of the stairs?" he asks.

"Yes," I say. "There are also bowls of water under the dining room table, in the laundry room, on top of the dresser in the guest bedroom, and under the bathroom sink."

"Why don't you just take her to the vet?" he begs.

I take her the next day. Returning home, I release the cat and stand in front of my husband.

"Well?"

"It's not good," I begin.

He puts a hand to his heart. "Oh my God. You mean she's…she's…"

"Oh, no, the cat's fine," I say, waving away his concern. "We're the ones in trouble." I pause, wondering how to relay the information I possess. I decide to just shoot it out there. "We have to wipe her butt. Daily."

He blinks. Opens his mouth. Thinks better of it. Opens it again.

"Why?" finally comes out.

"Because," I sigh. "She's too fat and her skin is folding over and trapping pieces of…you know…in the area of her—"

"Lalalalalalalalala," says my husband, sticking fingers in both ears. "I can't hear you. Lalalalalalalala…"

I give him "the look."

He removes his fingers. "Look here," he says. "You said cats were easy." He points an accusatory finger at me. "In fact, you *promised* that all we had to do was feed and water and occasionally pet them. And NOW," he raises his voice as I make to interrupt, "you're telling me we have to catch and hold down a creature—with claws—so we can wash poo from between the fatty folds of her butt?!"

51

"Um, actually," I say with a meek smile, "*you* have to wipe her butt. Poo makes me sick."

After several rounds of negotiations and the threat of divorce, I agree to at least hold the cat while he wipes.

I lull the cat into a false sense of security by combing her for twenty minutes. When she is relaxed and purring, I motion for my husband, hiding low at the top of the stairs with a wet towel, to approach.

"Is the towel the right temperature?" I whisper. "Not too hot and not too cold?"

He glares at me.

"Right," I say. "I'm sure it's fine."

Gingerly, as if afraid she was wired with explosives, he lifts the cat's tail. Her ears perk and she twists her head to look at him.

"Easy now," he says, wiping.

"*Mrow?*" queries the cat.

"I think she likes it," I encourage.

"That thought terrifies me," says my husband, prying open folds of fat to clean between them.

"*Rrrrrrrrr.*" The sound coming from her was half growl, half purr.

"Hurry up," I urge.

"Do you want this end of the job?" he asks. "Because I'm willing to trade."

We finish cleaning and my husband attempts to hand me the brown-stained cloth.

I make gagging noises and wave him away. "I can't even look at that."

"Well, what should I do with it?"

"Washing machine."

"Ewwww. I'm not putting kitty poo in the washing machine."

I look at him. "Please remind me to never bear you children," I say.

It got worse. I made the mistake of telling my mom about the butt-wiping. She was full of non-helpful suggestions.

"Maybe you need a bigger litter box. Maybe she just can't...you know...maneuver properly."

"The litter box is fine, Mom. The cat is just too fat."

"Well, I've never heard of such a thing. Everyone knows cats clean themselves."

"Mom, the vet said —"

"The vet! What does he know? What makes him such an expert?"

"Twelve years of schooling?" I reply.

I've stopped telling people we have to wipe the cat's butt. My friends with kids laugh at me. My friends without pets think I'm nuts. My friends with pets, especially cat owners, say nothing but look infuriatingly smug that they don't have to do the same.

So it's just me, the cat, and my husband bearing out our dirty little secret. It's almost become routine. Now every Monday, along with taking out the trash and watering the plants, we have the added chore of washing a weeks worth of kitty poo towels.

Yes, it's gross.

But at least the cat smells better.

Passion Denied

-9-

Passion Denied

My husband and I sit on the couch. We reach for one another. Kiss, kiss. Nudge, rub. Moans, giggles, and the beginning flickers of passion ignite. Until...

We have a sense of being watched. We open our eyes and she is sitting at our feet, staring at us. We ignore her and continue kissing. There is complete silence. We peek out from under our lids. She is still there. Staring.

"I can't do this with her watching," I say.

"Ignore her," says my husband, nuzzling my neck.

I accept his caresses, but keep looking back at the cat. She has plopped down on the carpet and is staring rapt at us, as if engrossed in a good movie. All she needs is a bowl of popcorn.

My husband senses my tension and stops. The cat looks from one of us to the other, eyes wide and innocent. *Don't mind me*, her look implies, *I'm not even here.*

We leave the cat and move into the bedroom. Kiss, kiss, kiss. An article or two of clothing hits the floor. Then we feel a plop at the foot of the bed. We look down and the cat is sitting on the corner of the mattress, staring at us.

"Nope," I say, getting up. "It's like performing in front of a camera. Can't do it."

My husband glares daggers at the cat, who, now that the show is over, starts to give herself a bath.

It's only recently the cat has decided to stalk us during foreplay. Her prior reaction was more like that of a child who catches their parents having sex. They do everything short of setting themselves on fire to erase the image from their mind.

Before, if the cat would see us kissing she would give a little start, as if we'd scared her. Then she would make a face and run off down the hall.

Eww, yuck. Stop it! That is sooo gross. Why would you want to do that?

Now I feel like we're the parents of a three-year-old, trying to find a moment when the child is distracted to sneak off and have sex.

"Psst. The cat's asleep on the window seat. Let's go."

So it lacks a little in the romance department. It gets the job done.

I think the cat wouldn't be so fascinated (or disgusted) by our open displays of affection if she weren't so standoffish herself. Getting her to agree to be petted is akin to entering into a trade agreement with a foreign country—

lots of conditions and clauses, and you're never sure if they're going to back out at the last minute.

To pet our cat, one must not have come into contact with any other animal in the past 48 hours. One must have warm hands, fresh breath, move slowly with no sudden movements, scratch diligently under her chin and behind her ears, and never under any circumstances touch her tail or paws. If any of these conditions are breeched, it can be taken as an all out declaration of war.

But perhaps I'm wrong. Maybe she is there to help, watching us with only the best intentions of offering advice. Perhaps her look of furrowed concentration comes from trying to send mental messages of encouragement to my husband.

Hey, scratch her behind the ear. We chicks love that. Now rub her tummy. And sort of pouf her hair up, and then pat it back down. That's sure to get her motor going.

The obvious solution would be to continue romantic activities behind closed doors. But many of the doors in our old home don't latch completely and, when fifteen pounds of kitty weight are thrown against them, they swing wide open.

Nowhere to run, nowhere to hide.

So we'll continue with the clandestine sex. Actually, it makes for a rousing change of pace. We feel a little naughty sneaking off behind the cat's back to do the wild thing.

And I must admit it's a whole lot more enticing than it was seeing the look of disgust on the cat's face when we so much as kissed.

Besides, it's not like nothing good has come from the cat watching us. Her presence has been inspiring, even.

I'm quite enjoying those tummy rubs.

Kitty Jihad

-10-

Kitty Jihad

I am scared for my life. Our three-year-old black and white female cat has declared Kitty Jihad on my husband and me. I'm unsure as to what provoked this kitty holy war, but my guess is it all started when the veterinarian had us reduce the amount of food we were feeding the cat. During the cat's last check-up, the vet had discreetly slipped me a brochure on caring for obese cats. I knew the cat's tummy had grown a bit, but obese? Ridiculous!

I showed my husband the brochure, hoping he would feel the same injured sense of outrage for our poor cat that I did. Instead, he started referring to her as "Tubby." If the cat was eating when he walked by he called out "Hey, Tubby, drop the nibbles and give me a lap!" He would then laugh roundly at this so-called humor. Neither the cat nor I was amused. I spoke with my husband about his insensitivity.

"She's not fat," I said. "The vet said she only needs to lose three pounds."

"Well, she weighs fifteen pounds. Three pounds is therefore approximately twenty percent of her body weight," he said smugly. "That's a lot." He turned to face the cat. "Isn't that right, Tubby?"

The cat made it clear she was not pleased with the new food rationing. I'm not making accusations, but let's just say I started finding kitty litter in a whole new variety of places around the house. But we stuck to our guns.

I laugh now at our naivety. I'd heard jokes about the sadistic and unforgiving nature of cats, but it wasn't until I became a cat owner with a ticked off cat that I was able to grasp the full sadistic implications of a feline's malice. Simply put, our cat has declared a holy war against us.

The Kitty Jihad focuses on sleep deprivation. Our cat, who must have studied at some institute of higher learning before we rescued her off the streets, has taken to intentionally interrupting our REM cycles during sleep. The REM (rapid eye movement) cycle is what is needed for deep sleep to occur. Without it, people become irritable, unfocused, and experience loss of memory and concentration.

It begins late at night, after we fall asleep. The cat leaps onto our bed, and stares at us, waiting for the jittery movement of the eyeball behind the closed lid, indicating deep sleep is now occurring. Then, and only then, does she hop to the floor, and position herself in the doorway between our bedroom and the hall. This is just beyond the distance, coincidentally, that either my husband or myself can throw a shoe or pillow with any accuracy.

Once positioned, the cat does some gargling and deep breathing exercises to prepare for what is to come. She inhales deeply into the depths of her lungs, and expels upward and outward a powerful burst of air that reverberates in the silence of the darkened house into one long, loud *"MEEE-OOOW!!"*

Once she sees my husband and I bolt upright in the bed, clutching frantically at the sheets, each other, and our pillows, she really lets rip. *"Meow, rowr, rowr, MOWW, mee-oooow."* Then she's silent. We hold our breath and wait. More silence. The worst appears to be over. We allow ourselves to fall back into our pillows.

"MROWRRRRR!!!!" screeches the cat at the top of her lungs.

"What the...?!?" my husband says, wrenching upright again.

"It's the cat," I say, punching the pillow and rolling over.

"Oh," he says. "I thought maybe you were being murdered by an intruder."

"No, but thanks for your concern," I mutter. "You almost made it fully out of the bed."

During this exchange, the cat has paced into the hallway. A twenty-minute silence allows us to return to sleep.

The cat again takes up position. Now she adopts a more lyrical, questioning tone of voice. *"Mrow? Rorw? Meow, meow."* Long pause. *"Mrow?"*

It's impossible to sleep through it.

I nudge my husband. "Honey, do you love me?" I ask.

"Mmm-um" he replies.

"Rowrrr? Mrreow?" says the cat.

I nudge him again. "If you really loved me you'd get up and do something about the cat."

He snorts air and pulls the covers tighter. "Uh-um. Didn' work lass night. Couldn't catch 'er." He begins to snore.

That's the signal the cat has been waiting for. "MROW!" she shrieks joyfully.

I carefully pry my husband off the ceiling.

What can we do? Kitty Jihad is declared and there is no escape. I've gotten out of bed to pet the cat but she just runs. I've plied her with toys to no avail. Finally I closed the bedroom door, but I'm not sure hearing muffled cat howls through painted wood is any sort of real victory.

We're barely holding our own. And although we're both on the verge of getting fired from our jobs—apparently it's frowned upon to use your keyboard as a pillow—we have not backed down. The time is coming though, when someone will have to give. As I left for work this morning, I noticed the cat. She was sitting oh-so-casually near our new sofa, flexing her claws.

"You wouldn't dare," I said.

She stretched and gave the couch a significant glance before strolling away.

So I'm ready to surrender. I just hope she doesn't do anything drastic before I get home from work. I'm worried though, because I might be a little late arriving.

You see, I'm going to have to stop and buy some kitty snacks.

Kitty Jihad wins again.

Part II
Cat & Kitten

A Second Cat

-11-

A Second Cat

I was worried about the cat.

She was lethargic, dragging around the house. Oh sure, she perked up when we fed her, scampering to her food dish, but otherwise she seemed bored.

I had the perfect solution.

"We need another cat," I told my husband.

He stared at me. "Are you insane?" he asked. "We can't deal with the one we've got."

"I know," I said. "But I think another cat would help. That way she would have a little friend to play with and she'd get some exercise. Plus, they can keep each other company while we're at work."

"Cats don't need company," said my husband. "They're independent."

He spoke in the same smug tone he uses when we discuss whether or not to leave a nightlight on for the cat. He insists there's no need, as cats can see in the dark. My point is that light is always a source of comfort, even if you can see fine without it. We never reached agreement on the matter and now take a passive-aggressive stance as we punch the nightlight over the stove on and off in a never-ending battle of will.

"Cats do need company," I argued. "Why do you think she follows me around when I get home from work? Because she's been alone all day and she wants to be around someone, that's why."

"That and you constantly feed her," my husband said.

We glare at one another.

"So are we getting another cat?" I ask.

"*No*," he said.

***

Two weeks later I sneak into the house. I've just returned from the vet where we take the cat once a month to have her claws trimmed. We did a price comparison and the six dollars we pay the vet tech to do this is much cheaper than the blood transfusions required each time we attempt it ourselves.

I release the cat from her carrier and she scurries off. I then carefully unwrap the bundle in my arms. It mews softly. My husband enters the room.

"What's that?" he asks, suspiciously.

"What?" I ask, looking over my shoulder.

"In your arms," he says speaking through clenched teeth. "What is that *in your arms*?"

I gently place the kitten on the floor and fling myself at my husband. I decided on the drive home the pity route was my best shot at victory.

"I was at the vet and I saw this kitten in a cage. *A cage!* And she is *so cute* and I *love* her and I think she would be a really good pet and the cat needs a friend and I love her and I can't take her back to that awful cage," I say, ending on a wail.

"No," he said.

I grab the kitten and wield her in front of his face, raising my voice to Minnie Mouse decibels. "Look how cute I am!" I coo, bouncing the kitten. "Look at my widdle face. Please don't send me back to the mean, old, ugly cage."

The kitten sends my husband a look. *Sorry man. Listen, is she always like this? Really, that cage wasn't so bad...*

My husband opens his mouth.

"Pleaseeeee" I say, shaking the kitten at him. She's looking a little dazed.

He rolls his eyes. "Fine, we'll see how it goes."

I knew exactly how it would go. Carrying the purring kitten home, I had visions of our two cats as compadres for life. They would bat a ball of yarn back and forth. Snuggle together side by side in front of a warm fire grate. Give each other baths. They would be the best of friends. And they would love *me* all the more for bringing them together.

The cat was peeking at the kitten from behind the kitchen door.

"Come here sweetie," I said. "Look what Mommy got for you." I picked the kitten up and placed her in front of the cat, waiting for the love fest to begin. I was, to say the least, unprepared for what happened next.

The cat's back rose in a boiling arch of fury as she towered over the kitten, spitting and hissing. Not to be outdone, the kitten arched her back and growled deep in her throat.

"Uh-oh," said my husband, taking a step back.

There was a flash of claws, flying fur, yelps, growls, and then it was over. The cat ran out of the room and the kitten crawled under the couch where she stayed for the next two weeks. The cat refused to speak to me for a month.

I was miserable.

"They hate me!" I wailed to my husband.

"Yes," he said.

I glared at him.

"You could be useful and help me fix this," I demanded.

"What?" he said. "You read the book. Just give them some time and space and they'll work it out on their own."

"What does a stupid book know?" I asked.

"The author is a doctor," said my husband.

"Big deal."

"She won an award."

"Shut up," I said.

I tried my own methods of reconciliation. Wedging myself under the couch, I managed to stroke a few stray hairs on the kitten's tail. I overfed the cat more than usual. But late at night I heard rumblings in the hall from the two cats that raised goose bumps on my spine.

The cats finally came around and deemed to be in the same room with one another. The cat stared, stricken, the first time the kitten played with her jingle ball, but she made no move to take it from her. Once the kitten realized the cat was more bluff than gruff, she ignored her.

My lot wasn't so pleasant. Since neither cat was pleased at the presence of the other, I continued to receive only lukewarm greetings from either of them. My husband's demeanor wasn't much better.

So it's up to me to mend this family rift. It will take time, patience, and perseverance, but I am up to the task. Besides, if I fail I have a back-up plan.

I saw an ad in the paper today for free puppies.
I can't lose.

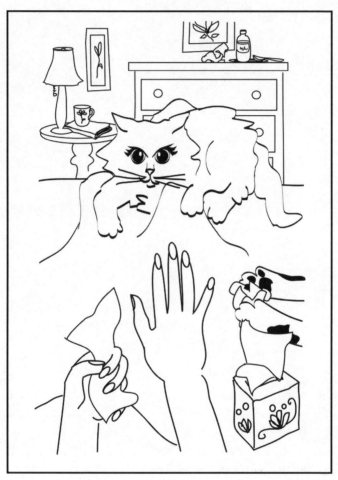

Kitty Nightingales

-12-

Kitty Nightingales

One Thursday night I came down with a bad cold.

I knew I faced a long night of tossing and turning, so I spared my husband my misery and opted to sleep in our guest bedroom. Miserably I sank beneath the sheets, making sure my two boxes of tissue were close at hand. My head was stopped up, my ears clogged, and it hurt to swallow.

I heard rustling and felt a soft "plop" as the kitten leapt onto the bed. She walked around my feet, a gentle purr emanating from her.

How sweet, I thought. *My baby senses I'm sick and she's here to comfor...*

I was stopped in mid-thought as my Nurse Nightingale kitten threw her body weight onto my foot, wrestling it under the covers and trying to bite through the comforter to subdue it.

"No, no!" I said, shooing her away. "Mommy's sick. No play time tonight."

I lay back and reached down to draw the covers up around my shoulders. Big mistake. The kitten leapt superman like in the air toward my extended arm.

"ROWR!" she announced with authority as she fell on it, battling it to submission.

"Hey, ow. Hey, stop that!" I said. "Go away. Go play with your sister."

Surprisingly, the kitten heeded my advice and went off in search of the cat. As I drifted off into a medicated sleep I could hear them chasing each other up and down the hall.

WHUMP! A kitten landed squarely on my chest. Before I found my breath to say anything she was off and running. But then, WHUMP! The older cat in hot pursuit (and a good ten pounds heavier than the kitten) also landed on my chest, knocking the wind out of me. They circled each other a few times on the bed while I gasped for air.

"Rowr, meow," said the kitten.

"Mrow!" warned the older cat, moving closer.

"Both of you shut up and get out of here," I wheezed.

The kitten went on the offensive and leapt over my thigh to swat at the cat. The cat saw it coming and jumped back, landing on my head. I shoved her off and she immediately darted for the kitten who meowed in delight and raced off the bed and back down the hall.

"I am going to throw you both out," I muttered. "Just as soon as I can stand up without feeling faint."

Eventually, after about three hours of wrestle-mania, both cats calmed down and decided they were ready for sleep. The kitten, still young enough to want to snuggle at night, found her way into my sickroom and curled up on my left side.

This brought the cat sniffing around. Independent, she has never slept with us. But she has been very aware of late of the need to keep up appearances as being just as cute and sweet as the new kitten. Seeing the kitten happily snuggled beside me the older cat sighed and plopped herself down on my right side. I was now sandwiched between two cats both of whom I found to be unnecessarily grumpy whenever I decided I needed to turn or roll over.

But the game of "I can do whatever you can" didn't end there. The kitten decided to give herself a bath, so the cat followed suit. Now I was surrounded, unable to move, by two animals making disgusting smacking and gulping noises in the dark. I tried to send mental telepathy to my husband to race in with the NyQuil® and knock me out.

In the morning I stumbled bleary-eyed and red-nosed into the kitchen. My husband was whistling as he fixed himself breakfast.

"There she is!" he said. "How are you feeling? All better after a good nights sleep?"

I glare at him with one bleary, bloodshot eye. "We-are-getting-a-DOG," I said through clenched teeth.

He frowned. "Why would we do that?" he asked.

"Because I need one to help me take the cats out, that's why," I said, slamming my cereal box on the counter.

The cats glide into the room, purring and rubbing against my husband's ankles. "Oh, whatta matter?" he asked, picking up the kitten. "Is Mommy in a bad mood?"

The kitten playfully batted his chin. The older cat looked on, beaming. My husband reached down to scratch her under her chin.

"Is Mommy being fussy? Yes she is. But who's a good girl? Who are daddy's good girls?" The cats have halo's glowing atop them.

My husband kissed me gently on the forehead. "You're still just feeling a bit under the weather," he said. "Don't take it out on the cats." He grabbed his briefcase and waved as he walked out the door.

I perched thoughtfully on the edge of the kitchen chair as I considered my options. I know what I have to do. It will have to be a really big dog.

I'm going to have to take my husband out too.

Kitty Nightingales

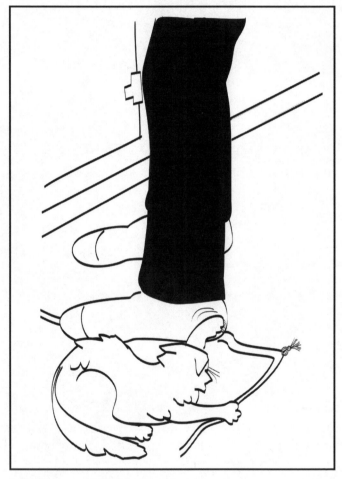

Dibbs!

-13-

Dibbs!

Having two cats is like having two children where you must never, ever, bring something home for one without buying the exact same thing for the other. Unfortunately, our cats are a bit on the greedy side. So even when we bring home something that is not for them, but rather for us, the cats still claim ownership.

For example, we brought home a new throw rug for the kitchen floor. Nothing fancy, just a basic woven throw with tassels on the ends.

We laid it on the floor.

"What do you think?" I asked my husband.

"Looks good," he said. "I —"

A rumbling, rushing sound filled the air as two cats careened around the corner. Eyes bulging, ears laid flat, feet racing, they were neck in neck in the home stretch. Then, in a surprise move, the kitten took a Herculean leap, passing the cat and was the first to land victoriously on the new rug.

"*Mrrowr!*" she screeched, spread-eagled across the fabric.

"Rowr-rrrr!" the cat yelped, looking to us as if for a judge's call. She screeched to a halt at the edge of the rug as if an invisible barrier protected it.

The kitten smirked as she pranced around the perimeter of the new rug.

"Well, it was nice for the thirty seconds we could call it ours," said my husband. "I'm going to watch TV."

I glared at his retreating back. Yet again, I was left to single parent the situation. Fortunately, I had the deft touch.

"You share," I told the kitten. "Be a good kitty. Share."

The kitten's idea of sharing was to settle into the middle of the rug and begin cleaning her private parts. I decided parenting was overrated and joined my husband in front of the TV.

The kitten made herself at home, not moving for the next two hours. Our entering the kitchen didn't deter her in the least, and she went so far as to let us step over and around her as we fumbled through trying to cook and set the table.

My husband, however, made the mistake of standing on the rug as he stirred something at the stove.

A rumble emanated from deep in the kitten's throat.

"I'd move if I were you," I told him.

"Why?" he asked.

The kitten walked over and glared at the portion of his shoe on the mat.

"You're on somebody's turf," I said.

He looked down at the scowling kitten. "I pay the mortgage," he said. "If I want to stand on my new rug, in my kitchen, no eight pound cat is going to stop me."

I shrugged and went back to rinsing off lettuce.

The kitten nudged his ankle with her head. When subtlety didn't work, she went for an all out head-butt.

"Hey, cut that out," said my husband.

The kitten whipped out her claws and targeted his sock, which unfortunately had his foot in it at the time.

"Ow. Hey. OW!" He hopped off the rug.

"Us, zero. Cats, 391," I said. My husband glared at me.

The cat moped in the doorway, watching the kitten nap on the rug. But older and wiser, she bided her time.

Per routine, I fed the cats at five o'clock.

The cat sashayed over and planted herself in front of the kitten's dish. The kitten sat up, alarmed. The cat smiled, and then sank her head deep into the kitten's food.

"Rowr, rowr, psst!" yelled the kitten. My husband and I came into the kitchen. The kitten stared accusingly at the cat. "Mrow, mow, mow!"

"Well, go get your food then," I said.

The cat hummed as she paroled the perimeter of the rug.

The kitten bit her lip and lay down on the mat.

The cat wasn't through. She started splashing around in the water dish. *Hear the water? When is the last time you went to the bathroom? Ho, hum. Splash, splash. I love playing in the runny water.*

The kitten crossed her legs. She looked worried.

Splish-splash. Splish-splash. Oh, how I love the runny, full, wet, drippy water.

The kitten turned a deep shade of purple as she held her breath. Unable to bear it any longer, she tore off the rug toward the litter box. Doing her business in record time, she raced back to the mat, coming to a dismayed stop at the edge.

The cat squatted at the corner of the rug, flipping a tassel back and forth.

Do you mind? her expression said to the kitten. *I'm getting ready for bed.*

Me, I'm fed up. It's impossible to be in the kitchen with territorial cats nipping at my heels and both cats toying alternatively with starvation and kidney implosion so as not to lose their claim on the rug to the other.

"We have to take action," I tell my husband.

He sighs. "You're right. We've spoiled them. But with hard work and commitment on our part, I'm sure we can teach them to do better."

I stare at him. "What?"

He stares back. "Weren't you going to lecture me that we need to find new ways of reward and discipline, so as to create a more fair, harmonious environment where we all learn a lesson about love and sharing?"

"Uh, *no*. I was going to suggest we go buy two small, crappy rugs for the hall and let them duke it out there."

He thought for a moment. "Okay, that's good too."

Too bad we don't have kids. We'd make great parents.

Dibbs!

El Toro Gato

-14-

El Toro Gato

I am envious of other people and their cats. Oftentimes it's their close relationship and sometimes it's just that their cats seem so...normal.

I was at a friend's home the other day when a fluffy black and white cat with a jingling ball tied around its collar presented itself.

"Oh, how cute," I said. "I have a tuxedo kitty too."

"Watch this," said my friend. She got down on all fours and the jingling kitty bounced over to her and they gently bumped heads.

"We used to just rub noses but now she likes to head butt me," said my friend. She beamed at the El Toro cat. "Isn't that *sweet?*"

This got me thinking. Why doesn't my cat perform cute tricks like that? She barely deems to let me touch her. As I drove home, I became more indignant. What was going on here? I pay for the food. I scoop up the kitty litter. I replace my sofa cushions monthly. I, too, deserve a head-butt.

The cat knew something was up the minute I walked in the door. This may or may not have had something to do with me immediately throwing my briefcase and purse on the table and dropping to the floor in front of her, arms splayed across the hall to prevent her untimely escape.

"Hi baby," I said, easing my head down toward her. "Nice kitty..."

My ophthalmologist tells me I am healing nicely and should be able to remove the eye patch within the month.

There's a woman who writes a gardening column for the small town papers in our area. It's the type of column I usually avoid reading as it involves things I know nothing about (dirt, nature, and enjoying dirt and nature), and never covers items I am interested in (how to air condition outside air or if it's socially acceptable to plant fake flowers outside and try to pass them off as real).

In a recent column, this writer wrote about tales of animal heroism...three ants that worked to dislodge a splinter from the body of a fourth; mother dolphins that stayed with their babies trapped in fishermen's nets, singing to them until both mother and infant drowned; and a group of sparrows that *picked up* a wounded sparrow and flew it off a busy street and into a city park. Anyone reading her article would come away with the understanding that animals are much more caring and compassionate then their human counterparts.

This woman needs to be introduced to my cats.

If I was lying stranded and bleeding in a net or on a busy street, the only reason my cats might be bothered to notice is if my mortal injuries delayed their feeding time. Then they might nose me a bit in the hopes of encouraging me to get up and open the canister that contains their food before I expired.

But this implies my cats go outside, which they don't. They've gotten so prissy they don't even try to hide the wrinkling of their nose, indicating distaste for my non-pleasing odor when I come in after a run. They are aghast that my parent's dog will not only come near me but *lick* me when I am in this state. I see their stares of horror and try to explain it to them.

"She likes the salt," I explain as the dog works her way up my arm.

The cats aren't buying it. They walk away, tails in the air. I can hear their unspoken thoughts. *That is just so uncouth and frankly, unsanitary. When is the last time that beast had her shots?*

I hope they are referring to the dog and not to me.

Another friend walks her cat on a leash. "He loves it," she brags. "He sits still whenever I get the harness out."

I passed this information on to my husband.

"NO," he said.

"No what?" I asked.

"No, we are not harnessing the cats," he answered.

"I didn't say I wanted to," I said. "I was just telling you..."

"And you can't make me," he said crossing his arms.

"What? I never..."

"You can't make me and I will leave you if you try to make me," he said. "I'm a person too and I have rights and one of my rights is to not knowingly place myself in harms way."

I rolled my eyes. "For heaven's sake, I didn't mean..."

He held his hand up, palm facing me. "I'm sorry," he said. "That's my final word."

I sighed. "Well, okay, if you feel that strong, I guess you win. We won't harness the cats."

"*Really?* I won? I never win. Wow. I won. That's great." A smile broke over his face and he wandered off toward the kitchen.

Well, what the heck. It just gives me more bargaining power for our next discussion. Which I happen to know centers around an agonizing amount of back work for him and a new garden for me.

Harness, indeed.

El Toro Gato

Bath Time

-15-

Bath Time

Pots and pans flew, foundations rattled, and howls reached the heavens.

It was time to bathe the cats.

"Bloody hell," growled my husband, attempting to hold a snarling cat under the waterspout. The kitten had knocked the kitchen phone off the hook and was frantically trying to reach PETA.

"You got it, you got it," I encouraged my husband from across the room. I didn't dare get any closer for fear of being mauled.

This was the ultimate exercise in stupidity. Everyone knows cats bathe themselves. But I'd read a magazine article that touted the benefits of semi-annual bathing and decided our cats deserved only the best. And for this decision, my husband's life now stood in danger.

"Come here and help me," he barked.

The drenched cat's eyes glowed a malevolent red. She'd been around long enough to suspect the reason she was wet and miserable in the first place probably originated with me. Now as she heard me summoned, an evil grin spread across her face.

"Um, maybe not," I said, backing against the wall.

"I've got to get the rest of these suds off her," he begged. "Now please, come here."

I reluctantly crossed the room. The cat flexed her right paw, extending and retracting the claw. I looked over to the corner where the kitten sat by the phone. She saw me watching her and immediately assumed the defensive Okinawa Crane pose from the *Karate Kid* movie. Back arched, she swayed on one foot, daring me to approach. No help there.

After ten minutes, four plastic cups, and a near-filing for divorce, we got the cat rinsed and released.

I turned to the kitten while my husband dabbed rubbing alcohol on his wounds.

"I'll take defense, you play offense," I told him, swatting his bottom in what I hoped was a gesture of encouragement. "Go get her, tiger!"

He abandoned dabbing and poured the alcohol over both arms, wincing.

"No. I'm not going back in."

"But we can't have only one clean cat!"

The look he gave me suggested I back slowly from the room.

I kept my distance from him, and the cat, who was none too pleased the kitten had escaped the watery ordeal. In fact, since this bathing episode I've awakened during the night with the feeling of being watched...or stalked. It turns out to be my cat perched beside me, waiting for the right moment to take revenge.

At least that's my take. My husband says I'm imagining things and the cat has long since forgotten about the bath, but I'm not so sure.

I may have the kitten teach me that Okinawa Crane technique.

Just in case.

Jingle Ball Horrors

-16-

Jingle Ball Horrors

As a responsible pet guardian, I make sure to keep up on the latest recommendations and innovations in pet care by reading the ripped and wadded up back issues of cat magazines at my vets every six months when I herd the cats there for their biannual shots.

The most recent article I read discussed the importance of playtime with your feline companions. Pets, the article emphasized, *love* and *rely* on playtime with their owners. It is a time of bonding and, if done regularly, will be something a pet looks forward to with excited anticipation every day.

See, here all along I had assumed our cats were happy stuffing their faces and then laying belly up in the sun for eight hour stretches. Little did I suspect that behind those full bellies and warm fur, kitty hearts were breaking because they did not have a regularly scheduled playtime with me. I set about to remedy the situation.

Walking in the door with purchases from the pet store, I felt confident one of the bags I held contained the secret to unlocking shared fun for me and my cats. I started out simple with their favorite toy from kittenhood, the cotton mouse.

"Here kitties," I said, dangling a bright yellow cotton mouse by its tail. "Come play."

The cat scratched her nose in her sleep and rolled over.

I tried the kitten. "See the mouse? Want to get the mouse?"

The kitten sat up and yawned. I was encouraged. At least one of them was awake.

I dug in the bag and pulled out rubber cheese.

"Oooooh," I exclaimed. "Look at the pretty cheese. Who wants to try and eat the pretty cheese?"

The kitten looked at the cat who gave a *I have no idea but just ignore her and maybe she'll leave* shrug.

I clapped my hands. "Hey," I announced. "You two are supposed to want to play with me, I bought all these toys, so guess what? We are going to play together. Now then."

I pulled two identical candy-cane striped jingle balls out of the bag. *Jingle, jingle. Jingle, jingle.* They made a happy noise.

The cats lay back down and turned their backs to me.

"Aw, c'mon!" I begged. "One round of chase the jingle ball. Here, I'll show you how."

And so it was I found myself rolling a jingle ball down the hallway and running after to retrieve and roll it again and again. I was panting when I returned to the cats after five rounds.

"See?" I huffed. "It's not so..."

But they were gone. I searched the house until I found the cat munching nibbles out of the kitten's dish and the kitten wedging herself under the dining room credenza in the hopes of hiding from me.

"Fine, you win," I said, abandoning the toys in the middle of the floor. "We won't play."

Cut to two AM and my husband and I warm under the blankets and deep in our dreams.

Jingle, jingle. Jingle, jingle.

My husband rolled over. "Wass' that?" he mumbled.

Jingle, jingle.

"I bought the cats some toys," I said. "They didn't like them. Just wait a minute and they'll quit."

Jingle, jingle. Jingle, jingle. Jingle, jingle. Jingle, jingle. Annoying, but bearable. Bearable that is, until the cats discovered how much better the balls sounded on hardwood floors.

JNGLE JINGLE. JINGLE JINGLE. JINGLE JINGLE JINGLE JINGLE JINGLE JINGLE JINGLE JINGLE JINGLE.

Pause.

JINGLE JINGLE JINGLE JINGLE JINGLE JINGLE JINGLE JINGLE.

Two hours later and there was no end in sight. Not only were the cats enthralled with their new playtime of "Chase the jingle ball," they also discovered a love of the game "Keep Away." As in every time we got out of bed to take the balls from them, they hid them somewhere unfindable, sitting and staring at us until we returned to bed. Then they retrieved the balls and reinstated soccer practice on the hardwoods outside our bedroom.

It's been a week, and I still can't find those jingle balls. The cats obviously have some secret hiding place they won't divulge. But I know they're out there. Because late at night, deep in the recesses of the house, drawing closer, we hear them coming.

Jingle, jingle.

Sometimes we hold each other and cry.

Those stupid pet magazines.

Jingle Ball Horrors

The Creature Under The Fridge

-17-

The Creature Under The Fridge

At first I didn't believe there was anything living beneath our refrigerator. I thought the cats were just messing with us.

But I reconsidered. We live in a large historic home and have had our fair run of mice over the years. Usually they enter through the large wooden cupboard next to the stove where we store our Tupperware®. But the cats weren't paying any attention to the cupboard. Their attention was focused under the fridge.

They prowled along the baseboards, sniffing so hard their bodies shook with the effort. Deep growls emanated from their throats. They would lie on the wooden floor, tails twitching, just watching, waiting.

I became wary of going near the fridge. All I could picture was a small, furry rodent scurrying over my bare foot in the morning as I reached for the orange juice. I started standing as far back from the door as possible and leaning my body in to grab whatever snack I needed before hurrying to the other side of the kitchen. The cats observed my discomfort and acted accordingly.

The next time I entered the kitchen, both cats were lying contently. But as I neared the fridge the older cat tensed her body, and scootched on her stomach closer to the fridge, peering intently beneath. Her tail whipped back and forth in warning.

"What is it?" I whispered. "Do you see the mouse?"

The cat gave me a we-have-a-situation-here look that indicated I could help most by shutting up. I scurried out of the kitchen.

The next day the kitten joined in the fun. The minute I stepped into the kitchen she raced toward the fridge and plunged both paws underneath. I leapt onto the countertop.

"What is it?" I cried. "Did you get it?" The kitten frowned and paced in front of the fridge. I decided breakfast wasn't that important of a meal and I would just skip it. Maybe forever.

And so it went. The cats stood guard for hours at a time. At night I would feel my way through darkened halls to the kitchen for a glass of water and there they were, waiting, their slanted eyes glittering in the pale moonlight filtering in through the window.

The cats refused to leave their guardposts, and the creature under the fridge grew in my mind to epic proportions of filth, hair, and malicious intent. I started giving the cats extra snacks to keep their strength up.

"Be good girls," I told them. "Catch the mouse for Mommy."

I spoke to my husband about calling in an exterminator. Or an army of them.

"What for?" he asked.

"To kill the creature under the fridge," I said.

"What creature?" he asked.

"Oh my God, are you blind?" I said. "The cats won't leave that spot. There is obviously some huge, horrible, fanged mutant mouse thing that has taken refuge in our home. Probably the only reason we haven't been eaten alive is because our babies are protecting us."

He smirked. "The only reason the cats sit there is because you feed them every time you walk by. If I'm the only one home, they just lie around the front room."

I stared at him, sure I heard wrong. Was he inferring that my babies would intentionally mislead me, purely for their own gain? But my husband is an intelligent and astute man, an honest man. It came down to having to believe the love of my life or thinking something slightly ill of my cats. It was a simple choice.

"You are full of it," I told him. "I'm telling you the cats are on the scent and there is something huge and horrible under there. Now please, call in the National Guard."

As we entered the kitchen, both cats snapped to attention. The older cat approached the fridge and growled. The kitten hissed and arched her back. Both peered hopefully up at me from the corners of their eyes.

Squatting on all fours, my husband peered under the fridge. Grimacing, he reached for the broom and raked out four bouncy balls coated in grime, two browned and wilted pieces of lettuce, 14 marbles (I don't even want to hazard a guess), three pieces of pasta, and a Christmas ornament we lost two years ago.

He started to get up, took a second look, and eased the broom back under the fridge. As he drew the broom toward us, I glimpsed something brown and dirty. Then the cats were upon it. All we could see were claws, ears, and tails. I screamed, my husband tried to pull the cats away, and marbles rolled everywhere. When the cats finally separated we looked down and saw...nothing. Whatever had been pulled out was now no more than a few stray wisps of cobweb, some lint, and lunch in our cats' stomachs.

"I told you so," my husband and I said at the same time.

He looked at me. "There was no creature."

I looked back. "There most certainly was. Did you not see the cats go berserk?"

"Yes, over an old mouse toy."

"Or a man-eating rodent."

"Was not."

"Was too."

"Was not."

"Was too."

The disagreement continues to this day. I suspect his insistence that there was nothing under the fridge is simply a manly cover to conceal his fear of the beast that almost destroyed us.

So I've explained to the cats that even if Daddy won't acknowledge it, we are both extremely grateful for their saving our lives from the horrible fanged mutant creature that surely lived under our fridge.

The Creature Under The Fridge

Can You See Me?

-18-

Can You See Me?

When she was little, my sister used to poke her fingers beneath the bathroom door and wiggle them.

"Can you see me?" she'd ask.

"Go away," whoever was inside would answer.

She would shove her hand further beneath the door.

"Now? Can you see me now?"

"Yes, I see you now. Can you please go away for a few minutes?"

The hand would disappear and there would be a light thud as she leaned her small body against the door.

"When are you coming out?"

We were all happy to see that phase end, and I thought my days of being stalked while on the toilet were over. I admit to giggling when friends moaned about how their children never left them alone, even when they were in the bathroom.

"Should've had cats," I informed them smugly.

But my life of bathroom solitude has been upended. Both cats have recently decided they can't abide a closed door, be it a closet door, bedroom door, or—you guessed it—bathroom door.

They scared the daylights out of me the first time. I woke in the middle of the night and felt my way to the bathroom. Half asleep, I sat on the toilet, when suddenly, "*Whump!*" The bathroom door flew open and a small tabby cat stood illuminated in the doorway. She gazed steadily at me before turning away. My heart raced. I felt like I'd been given a warning visit by the kitty Mafia.

Keep the door open, or else.

I alerted my husband the next morning. "Better lock the door when you're in the bathroom."

"Why? Is asking you to stay out not enough?"

"No, it's the cats," I said, looking over my shoulder. "They don't like closed doors."

"Uh-huh," he said slowly. "And I should be concerned...why?"

But Mister Oh-so-smart wasn't laughing when the cats body-slammed the bathroom door open while he was reading *Newsweek.* I was upstairs when I heard his call for help.

"Would you get the cats out of here?" he asked. "I can't do this with them watching."

So we started locking the door. That's when tiny paws began to appear underneath the door.

It was cute for a while. A tiny white paw would slide beneath the door and tap the floor.

Can you see me?

But then there was the talking. Finding the door wouldn't budge and unable to reach us from beneath the door, the cats would sit outside the locked door and "talk" to the person inside.

"Mrow. Rowr-rowr. Mow?"

When are you coming out?

The best though, was coming home early and finding both cats sitting outside the bathroom where my husband had locked himself in. He was talking back to them.

"Rowr? Meow, meow," said the cats.

"Yeah, I know. I hate when that happens," he answered through the closed door.

"Purr, rowr-meow."

"Really? So what did you tell them?"

"Mow! Psfft! Meow."

"Ah, ha ha," he said. "You are so clever."

"Honey?" I knocked. "Everything okay?"

There was a moment of silence. "I have no idea what you're talking about," he called back.

I wasn't letting him off that easy. I squatted on the floor and wriggled my fingers beneath the door. "Can you see me?" I asked.

"Go away," he growled.

I scratched on the door. "So when are you coming out?"

"The minute I do I'm having you committed," he warned. "Go away!"

And so it went. We had pretty much resigned ourselves to a life of potty-patrol, when luck struck. Running into the house one day, I dashed for the bathroom without bothering to close the door. No cats appeared. Excellent. I shared my discovery that night with my husband.

"I broke the code!" I said. "We need to adopt an opendoor policy. If you don't close the door, they take no interest in what you're doing in there."

He seemed less than thrilled. "But I like closing the door."

I sighed. "Pee with an audience outside a closed door or do your business in peace with an open one. It's your choice."

"I miss our life before cats," he said.

He has a point. It was nice when we had some say so over the ajar status of doors in our home. Still, even with all the bother, it's nice knowing you are so important to someone that every minute apart counts.

"*Mrow?*"

Yes, I'll be out soon.

Can You See Me?

Tacky Tape Sucks & Other Reasons I Can't Own Nice Furniture

-19-

Tacky Tape Sucks & Other Reasons I Can't Own Nice Furniture

Tacky Tape. Transparent, thin pieces of what is essentially two-sided tape which may be applied directly to fabric to keep cats from using furniture as sharpening posts. In bold letters on the package front it advertises that Tacky Tape "STOPS CATS FROM DESTROYING FURNITURE."

Right.

After spending twenty minutes removing the individual Tacky Tape strips from their brown base sheet and positioning the sticky side down on my furniture, then cracking and peeling the white application paper on top to reveal the exterior sticky side (Apparently you must have some sort of science degree to properly mount your Tacky Tape. Liberal Arts majors beware), I managed to end up surrounded by twenty balled up wads of Tacky Tape.

Miraculously, I managed to apply the last two strips to our twin library chairs where our cats love to sharpen their claws.

The idea of Tacky Tape is that when your cat reaches up to claw the chair their paw will stick to the tape. They will not enjoy this sensation and will be cured for life from any lingering desire to use said chair for sharpening their claws.

You betcha.

It almost worked on the kitten. She walked up to the tape and gave a hesitant sniff. She sat by the corner of the chair, unsure how to proceed. The cat had no such qualms. She marched up to the Tacky Tape and batted at it. This slight motion knocked half the Tacky Tape off the chair, so it was now fluttering like a banner in the wind. The cat went in for the kill, grabbed the fluttering end of the tape in her mouth and pulled the Tacky Tape ("STOPS CATS FROM DESTROYING FURNITURE") off the chair and onto the floor where she proceeded to make origami animals out of it.

We gave up on the Tacky Tape. (I was still incensed about the swan the cat made from the last ball of tape.) We had other things to worry about. Namely, our upcoming meeting with the designer who was to help us select fabric for our new couch.

The meeting started on a positive note. We explained to the designer we were looking for a couch that was both casual and elegant, something you'd feel comfortable lying on to watch TV or inviting guests to sit on. We spoke in hushed, modulated tones, and the designer nodded approvingly and said she had several beautiful fabrics she thought would meet our needs.

She brought the first one out and my husband and I exchanged a troubled glance. It was a weave pattern with tiny threads in crisscross stitches just begging to be plucked apart by sharp kitty claws. We exclaimed over the beauty of the fabric but said it wasn't quite what we were looking for.

No problem, said the designer. She returned with a stunning floral fabric of silk brocade flowers. She was raving about the timeless statement of classic elegance such a fabric boasted when I interrupted.

"Um, I don't think that's for us."

The designer kept her smile in place. "And why not?"

I gave a nervous laugh and looked at my husband who shrugged. "Well, you see, our cats would destroy the threads in those flowers before we even got the plastic off the couch."

"Ah, I see," said the designer, never losing her smile. "Well, we have many different fabrics so I'm sure we'll find the right one for you."

Two hours and fifty fabric samples later we left the designer in a sobbing huddled mass in the corner of her store. We had categorically rejected every piece she brought out. Too woven, too many threads, too much fringe, no tassels allowed, dark colors show cat hair. I knew it was time to leave when the designer presented us with a piece of burlap and wished us the best of luck.

So we sit at home and dream about the day when we'll be able to pick out furniture we actually like and not furniture designed to withstand World War III. Until then, we're taking the advice of designers everywhere and using accent pieces to try and dress up the house.

The Tacky Tape swan, in particular we feel, lends a touch of elegance to our home.

Morning Revelry

-20-

Morning Revelry

My husband and I consider ourselves adults. We hold jobs, pay bills, and brush regularly. Yet every morning at five AM we are forced to feign death in the hopes of catching just a little more shut-eye. Basically, we're two thirty-five year olds playing possum.

We lay side-by-side in bed, motionless, feigning deep-sleep breathing. Aware that each other is awake, but neither willing to admit it, we are careful not to roll over, cough, or show any sign of life.

The reason for us lying statue-like is a small, furry creature perched on a chair across from our bed, right under the windows. It is our kitten, who has decided she is hungry. She knows food is forthcoming only after one of the large two-legged creatures she lives with gets out of bed. Therefore, she is on a mission.

"Mrow," she says.

It's crucial not to be the first to move. The bed is soft and warm, the stakes are high. We make little smacking sounds with our lips, trying to convince the other we are really asleep.

The kitten hops off the chair, crosses the floor, and leaps onto the bed, which is to my advantage. I love the feel of a small cat crawling over me. My husband, on the other hand, does not.

She purrs around our heads, encouraging us to wake up. I don't move. I feel my husband clench and unclench his fists. Sitting up, he deposits the kitten on the floor. He punches his pillow and quickly lies back down.

Wife – 1, Husband – 0.

Having seen signs of life, the kitten is encouraged. She hops back up on the chair and starts batting the wooden window blinds against the glass. The bedroom vibrates with the reverberations.

After a few minutes of the wooden blind death rattle, the kitten appears to have given up. There is silence. We both relax and start to drift back into real sleep.

"*Ka-ching, ka-ching, ka-ching.*" She's back, having located her jingle ball and nudged it into our bedroom. She is now under our bed, racing in circles as she chases it around. "*Ka-ching, ka-ching, ka-ching.*"

I bite my lip and taste the sweat there. She's good.

The noise of the jingle ball has brought the cat on the run. She's constantly afraid we're playing with the kitten and forgetting to include her. She breathes a sigh of relief when she sees the kitten playing solo and two lumps still tucked in bed. Unfortunately, seeing us tucked in and comfortable reminds her she's hungry too, and the cats decide to double-team us.

The cat takes over jingle ball duties (*ka-ching, ka-ching, ka-ching*), while the kitten hops back up to the blinds. (*Rattle-rattle. Rattle-rattle.*)

The bedroom is a cacophony of noise: *Ka-ching, rattle-rattle, ka-ching, rattle rattle. Ka-ching, rattle, ka-ching, rattle.*

I can't stand it any more. "Shut up!" I yell at the cats.

My husband's voice comes muffled from under the covers. "You spoke first. You lose. Go feed them so I can get some sleep."

I rip the covers off him. I am not in the best of humor in the mornings, especially at five AM.

"*You* were the one who sat up and put the kitten on the floor so technically you were awake first and you should be the one to get up."

"If you heard me put the kitten on the floor that means you were awake and just pretending to be asleep, which is a terrible thing to do, so *you* should be the one to get up."

"No, you."

"No, you."

"Mrow-rowr!!" wail both cats. They pick up the pace. *Ka-ching-rattle, ka-ching-rattle.*

I hold my hands over my ears and glare at my husband. "Get up."

He pulls the covers up and rolls over. "Eat dirt."

I lay back down. "If you're not getting up, I'm not getting up."

We lie in bed and glare at the ceiling. There is no hope of either of us getting any more sleep.

I turn my head and look at my husband. "Together on the count of three?"

He nods.

"One..."

We roll the covers back.

"Two..."

We both put a foot on the floor and look suspiciously at one another.

"Three!" He stands up and I fling myself back into bed.

Wife - 2, Husband — 0.

An hour later guilt overtakes me and I pad out to the kitchen where he is sitting and put my arms around him, kissing the top of his head.

"How about if I promise to be the one to get up and feed the cats tomorrow?" I ask.

"That's what you said yesterday."

I sigh. He's right. My intentions are good, but when it's 5 AM and cold and dark outside the warmth of the bed, I know I will once again feign death in the hopes he'll get up first. And he'll do the same.

But we are united on one front.

The cats are comatose on the couch, satiated and asleep. We sneak up behind them and on the count of three I rattle the blinds while he wings a jingle ball along the floor.

The cats hit the ceiling.

That's right, baby. Score one for the humans.

The End

Credits

Feline Concerns first appeared in I Love Cats! Magazine (www.iluvcats.com).

Lessons In Stalking first appeared in the ASPCA Animal Watch newsletter.

Kitty Jihad, Dibbs!, Never Feed A Cat Grape Benadryl®, The Creature Under the Fridge, Morning Revelry, Kitty Nightingales, El Toro Gato, Yoga Cat, The Great Cat Butt Wiping Adventure and *The Big Brown Mouse & Other Toys Our Cat Loathes* all originally appeared in Cats & Kittens (www.catsandkittens.com) magazine.

Afterword

Toward the completion of this book my cover and interior layout designer, Robert Howard, suggested it would be a nice touch to include a "family portrait" of my husband, myself, and our two cats at the back of the book.

"Did you read my book?" I asked. "Were there any stories in there that might lead you to believe such an undertaking is even remotely possible?"

"Try anyway," came the reply. And so, risking life and limb, we did.

You see the results below. We never actually managed to get all four of us in the room at the same time. In a rare show of unity, one cat would distract us while the other made her getaway. After an hour of this we decided one photo each of me with the cats would suffice. To clue you in to how *that* process went, what you are seeing here is the best of the best—me holding Lucy captive against the floor as I lay on her and Olivia looking anxiously at the floor, planning her escape. Blair, my husband, remains in safe (and, one might add, unscratched) anonymity behind the camera lens.

Robert's only comment was "Next time try Tuna Fish on your breath."

If you'd like more information (and photos!) on the cat, the kitten, and the inside story on *Lessons In Stalking*, please visit us at www.lessonsinstalking.com.

About the Author

Dena Harris is a humorist and freelance writer published in newspapers, magazines, and web sites around the country. Publication credits include *Chicken Soup for the Cat Lover's Soul, Cats & Kittens* magazine, *I Love Cats!, Puppies USA, Writer's Digest, The Toastmaster, Art Jewelry, Self-Publishing Essentials,* and more.

She teaches seminars and workshops in public speaking, networking, and writing for magazines. Her next book, *Scared Speechless: Public Speaking Tips For The Occasional Speaker,* will be available in 2006.

Raised in Ohio, she now lives with her husband and two cats in rural North Carolina and is constantly trying to figure out how to bring a third cat into the home without her husband's knowledge.

She is a member of the Cat Writer's Association (CWA), the Society for Children's Books Writers and Illustrators (SCBWI), the Writer's Group of the Triad, and way too many book clubs. For information on her upcoming books and workshops, please visit www.denaharris.com.

About the Illustrator

Linda Santell is a digital artist, designer and illustrator. She lives in the historic district of a small town in rural North Carolina, where her studio is also located. The slow, quiet environment serves as a great balance to her whirring, creative spirit.

Linda specializes in creating completely custom images, designs and illustrations. Her work is original and contemporary. She works equally well in color and black and white.

Her client base is primarily creative, entrepreneurial women—an eclectic mix of writers, small business owners and non-profits. She delights in supporting them in designing their dreams.

Illustration is Linda's second career, but her first love. Art became her full-time focus in 2000. Her projects range from book illustration to logo design, custom invitations to pet portraits and beyond.

Linda finds great joy in creating her own art, which often takes the form of colorful and whimsical illustrations with supportive messages for women. These illustrations have become the basis for her Whimsical Wisdom® line of women-centered art and products.

To learn more about Linda, her art and creative services, visit her at www.lindasantell.com or her sister site www.enrichingearth.com.

Comical Cat Cards

Dena & Linda have picked
some of their favorite
illustrations from

"Lessons in Stalking"
to make available
as note cards .

For more about the cards,
visit Linda at **www.lindasantell.com**

For more about Dena visit:
www.denaharris.com

Order Form for Lessons in Stalking

If you would like extra copies of Lessons in Stalking, you can order on-line at www.lessonsinstalking.com (credit card payments available) or use this order form.

For quantity orders (10+) please call 206-203-1154 or e-mail us at spotlightpublishing@triad.rr.com.

I'd like to order_____ (number of copies)

I've enclosed_____ ($9.95 per book + $2.50 shipping and handling)

Make Check Payable and Send Order Form To:
    Spotlight Publishing, Inc.
    PO Box 621
    Madison, North Carolina, 27025-0621

Ship to:
Name_____
Address_____
City_____State_____Zip_____

Please allow 2 weeks for delivery of your order

Want an autographed copy? It will be my pleasure to provide you with one. Simply make a note below, telling me how the inscription should read, and it will be provided to you at no cost.

To:_____
Special Instructions/Requests: _____
_____
_____

Ready for more of the cat and kitten? Then be the first in line for the hilarious sequel:

Do You Live Here Too?
More Life With Cats

Including the stories:
- Kiss my Kitty Butt
- Bug Patrol
- Let Me At The Twittering Things
- Thy Vacuum Is Mine Enemy
- Kitty Stand Off at the O-Cat Corral

To place your name on the pre-publication mailing list (no obligation to order, you'll simply receive an e-mail when the book is available for purchase), please send an e-mail to:

spotlightpublishing@triad.rr.com with the SUBJECT heading: More Life With Cats